We're Christ's representatives.

God uses us to persuade men and

women to drop their differences

and enter into God's work of

making things right between them.

We're speaking for Christ

himself now: Become

friends with God;

he's already a friend with you.

2 Corinthians 2:20 (Message)

Expanding the Expedition Reach
Through

Marketplace Multipliers

Wayne Schmidt
Carrie Whitcher
Kay Kotan

EXPEDITION

Expanding the Expedition Reach Through

Marketplace Multipliers

By Wayne Schmidt, Carrie Whitcher, and Kay Kotan

©2021 Market Square Publishing, LLC

books@marketsquarebooks.com
141 N. Martinwood Road   Knoxville, Tennessee 37923
ISBN: 978-1-950899-34-0

Printed and Bound in the United States of America
Cover Illustration & Book Design ©2021 Market Square Publishing, LLC
Publisher: Kevin Slimp
Editor: Kristin Lighter

**Unless noted, Scripture quotations taken from
the following version of the Holy Bible:**

NIV

Scriptures marked NIV are taken from THE HOLY BIBLE,
NEW INTERNATIONAL VERSION ®.
Copyright ©1973, 1978, 1984, 2011 by Biblica, Inc.™.
Used by permission of Zondervan.

This resource was commissioned as
one of many interconnected steps in the
journey of *The Greatest Expedition.*

GreatestExpedition.com

Table of Contents

Foreword

This resource was commissioned as one of many interconnected steps in the journey of *The Greatest Expedition*. While each step is important individually, we intentionally built the multi-step Essentials Pack and the Expansion Pack to provide a richer and fuller experience with the greatest potential for transformation and introducing more people to a relationship with Jesus Christ. For more information, visit GreatestExpedition.org.

However, we also recognize you may be exploring this resource apart from *The Greatest Expedition*. You might find yourself on a personal journey, a small group journey, or perhaps a church leadership team journey. We are so glad you are on this journey!

As you take each step in your expedition, your Expedition Team will discover whether the ministry tools you will be exploring will be utilized only for the Expedition Team or if this expedition will be a congregational journey. Our hope and prayer is *The Greatest Expedition* is indeed a congregational journey, but if it proves to be a solo journey for just the Expedition Team, God will still do amazing things through your intentional exploration, discernment, and faithful next steps.

Regardless of how you came to discover *The Greatest Expedition,* it will pave the way to a new God-inspired expedition. Be brave and courageous on your journey through *The Greatest Expedition!*

Kay L Kotan, PCC
Director, *The Greatest Expedition*

Introduction

Earl works in the federal government in Washington, DC. Among his work responsibilities is to be sure people with disabilities have full access to technology. A co-worker shared with Earl that he is agnostic, that he does not believe in God. Earl simply said, "I'm going to pray that God will show Himself to be real to you." Sometime later, when discussing weekend plans, the co-worker shared he was planning to go to church that weekend. He went on to share that God was becoming real to him – and he eventually committed his life to Christ.

Yare is a global marketing director for a large pharmaceutical company – she travels the world. While in Europe she noticed a colleague seemed especially burdened. When Yare asked how she was doing, her colleague shared the burdens she was carrying. Yare asked permission to pray for her, and the colleague agreed – opening up the opportunity for further spiritual conversation.

Laura is a hair stylist. She sees clients on a regular basis in a setting where it is easy to talk about almost everything. Those clients know she cares about them personally and not just their appearance. This has opened the door for her to listen to them, express a willingness to pray for them, and to share her own testimony with them.

Jeff coaches basketball at a Christian university. He recognized that the 12 players on the team were the same number of disciples Jesus invested in. He and his coaching colleagues encouraged an "I am third" approach to basketball and life – God first, others second, I am third. Their basketball success has led to many others asking for some of the secrets to their success, which gave the coaching staff the opportunity to share about spiritual discipleship as well. Their sphere of influence now includes public as well as Christian educational institutions, at the high school, college and professional levels. He's committed to excellent basketball, but most energized by making disciples, who in turn are making disciples.

Sharon brings leadership and training skills to her role in HR in a banking corporation. With the permission of her employers, she has offered an optional prayer time to employees. It's become a place where employees can bring their prayer requests and know that people in their company care about them as a person as well as their performance. Sharon's discernment of the needs of others has given her opportunity to share the Gospel.

Rochelle is a nurse who has launched a gathering for spiritually seeking co-workers. Phillip is an engineer and defense scientist for the Department of National Defense in Canada, who is passionate about connecting faith and science. Julia is Chief Operating Officer for a community hospital, and intentionally integrates her management responsibilities with spiritual care and investment in her employees, resulting in commitments to Christ. Omar owns an insurance company that especially focuses on the needs of those living in geographical areas prone to hurricanes, and his commitment to go the extra mile gives him the opportunity to share about Jesus. Estherlita's consulting business addresses not only the IT needs of corporations, but leads to conversations of spiritual significance.

The names have not been changed, the accounts are not fictional, and these are not actors. These are real people working real jobs that you can read or hear more about by visiting www.marketplacemultipliers.com.

The list could go on, including people in blue collar and white collar workplaces, people with different personalities, and a variety of marketplace roles.

With so much difference in who they are and where they work, what do they have in common? They view their work as more than a job. It's a calling. They have a sense of being blessed and sent by their local pastors and churches into their everyday "mission fields." They want to learn more about integrating their faith with their work as disciples of Jesus, and stewarding their influence to help others become fully devoted followers of Christ. They are marketplace multipliers (MM).

There is a growing "gospel gap" across North America and around the world. More people than ever do not have the opportunity to make an informed decision about Jesus or even know personally a follower of Christ. While we're grateful for every spiritually interested seeker who begins their exploration by visiting a local church, much more often it is in the everyday places of life that they come into contact with those who winsomely and fully follow Christ.

There has never been a significant

movement of God without the significant engagement of lay people. When laypeople partner with pastors, the potential for Kingdom advancement intensifies. This leads to disciples making disciples (discipling disciples), people being empowered in faith, and equipped to grow so that God's Spirit fills every part of them and ripples out into the lives around them.

We believe the marketplace, where believers and those yet to believe cross paths every day, provides an intersection for a multiplication movement.

We join with others who are inspired by *The Greatest Expedition.* As co-authors we are partners not only in this booklet about Marketplace Multipliers, but seek to be one example of "clergy and laity" partnering together in order to fulfill the Great Commission to "Go and make disciples..." We believe the "Go" in Jesus' words calls the Church to be increasingly sending MMs who are providentially positioned in a variety of

workplaces to be increasingly unleashed to
make disciples in order to extend the Gospel
beyond the walls of the Church and to the ends
of the earth.

What began informally and conversationally
is now finding expression with intentionality
and action. What was birthed in prayer is now
becoming reality as we pursue it with purpose.
At this point an emerging MM movement is
very much a Kingdom "mustard seed,"
modest beginnings with seemingly unending
possibilities.

I (Carrie) am a follower of Jesus and a
Marketplace Multiplier. I have worked in the
healthcare field for over 20 years in a variety
of settings – a multi-hospital health care
system, skilled nursing, and rehabilitation
facilities. And for the last 16 years, I've
worked at a health care insurance company
in upstate New York where I serve as the Vice
President of Health Care Improvement. As I
became a follower of Jesus at a young age and
was raised in a faithful family, inclusive of a

younger sister with special needs, I have been called to serve others and make a positive, lasting impact on those I encounter in the marketplace. Improving health care is a never-ending journey requiring resilience, boldness and a deep desire to put others' needs over your own. It also requires mature faith to trust in His plan and seek His wisdom. I strive to use my influence to integrate my faith in all that I do and with all whom I encounter every day.

I (Wayne) am a follower of Jesus and an ordained minister in The Wesleyan Church. For over 40 years, I've been privileged to serve in three primary contexts: for three decades as co-founder and pastor of Kentwood Community Church, then six years providing leadership to Wesley Seminary at Indiana Wesleyan University in its early formative years, and since 2016 as General Superintendent of The Wesleyan Church. In each of these contexts, while called personally to vocational ministry, I have been a passionate proponent of the priesthood of all believers and an active supporter of those whose primary calling is fulfilled in the marketplace.

I (Kay) am a fourth generation United Methodist serving the church from a laity role ranging from coach, consultant, contractor, congregational developer, jurisdictional delegate and serving on denominational conference cabinets. My spiritual journey, like many others, has encountered multiple detours, valleys and mountain top experiences. Ultimately, I have discerned a call to ministry from a not too traditional role continuously empowering laity and challenging all leaders to make disciple-making disciples.

The story of Marketplace Multipliers unfolds in the following pages. This Journey is emerging from its launch phase to multiplication of MMs within local churches and around the world. The Journey we describe has its challenges – "You can have a mess without movement, but you can't have a movement without some mess." We'll share the highest hopes of those leading the MM initiative as well as very practical ways in which it functions within local churches.

CHAPTER ONE

The Need for Marketplace Multipliers

There is a growing "Gospel Gap" around the world and particularly in North America. More people than ever do not have the opportunity to make an informed decision to follow Jesus. Of those who at some point in their lives have expressed an intent to follow Jesus, many have compartmentalized their faith so it is limited to occasional religious activities, or have developed a consumer mentality where the focus is only on their needs. They have not experienced the joy of deeper discipleship that pervades all dimensions of their lives.

We love our pastors and we love our local churches. We celebrate the making of disciples taking place within the walls of the Church.

But many of us on *The Greatest Expedition* journey realize that the Gospel Gap will only be bridged if every person in their everyday lives is consistently encouraged to integrate their faith with their work and be a winsome influence for Christ in the lives of others. It is a faith adventure for all of us in all contexts... carrying the Good News beyond the walls of the Church.

Increasingly people's first exposure to the Gospel (has not and) will not be in visiting a church in person. We must leverage the already existing life-on-life environments like those found in the marketplace. The marketplace environment provides opportunities for people to establish a relationship with Jesus through the example and influence found in the relationships they develop in daily environments with MMs.

This is the way the Gospel has spread since the birth of the Church recorded in the book of Acts. It is true the Gospel was shared by people like the Apostle Paul in the synagogues and in that context Jewish individuals came to know Christ. Every day Paul and other co-workers in Christ maximized their marketplace connections to share good news.

Two of Paul's closest co-workers, Aquila and Priscilla, also had a tent making business. "After this, Paul left Athens and went to Corinth. There he met a Jew named Aquila, a native of Pontus, who had recently come from Italy with his wife Priscilla, because Claudius had ordered all Jews to leave Rome. Paul went to see them. Because he was a tent-maker as they were, he stayed and worked with them" – (Acts 18:1-3).

Together, Priscilla and Aquila owned and worked in their family retail business. They were fully partners in work and marriage. In the six references where both are mentioned, the name of Priscilla comes first in three instances and Aquila in the other three. Their work positioned them to share their faith because their business could function in a variety of locations where they could reach out to new people in new communities. The paths of the missionary journeys can be connected to the trade routes and business centers of their day.

When not preaching and teaching, we can imagine Paul, Aquila, and Priscilla sitting together in Aquila's shop as they plied their needles and fashioned or repaired tents. Aquila and Priscilla shared the duties of their workshop. This must have added to Paul's joy in partnering with Aquila and Priscilla for he was of the same craft, and at times supported himself in this way.

They recognized the value of manual toil. They were likely proud of their craft and that the product of their joint labors was known for its excellent quality. This seems to have given Aquila and Priscilla a wide-reaching positive reputation. They were in the tent business first and foremost to give glory to God.

If you were to visit the ruins of Corinth today, it is evident the location of the market street would have placed them strategically in the heart of the community. Your guide would describe how people would walk through the marketplace and stop in the shops. In your imagination you could see a tent-making business where people not only received an excellent value through their purchases, but had an opportunity to learn about so much more beyond tents.

Paul, with Priscilla and Aquila in partnership, catalyzed a disciple-making movement in the synagogue and marketplace. What if their witness had been limited to just the synagogues? How would this have impacted the quantity of people who would have heard the Gospel and the ethnic variety of people (Jews and Gentiles) who would have been invited to respond?

The *both/and* relationship of the synagogue and marketplace in biblical times is a model for us today. Sacred spaces and everyday places are both contexts for not only making disciples, but is the very place where discipleship multiplication can begin and grow into a movement once again.

CHAPTER TWO

The Movement Begins

Marketplace Multipliers (MM) is a *beyond-the-walls-of-the-church* disciple-making movement. MMs are rooted in their local church and sent out by their church. Just as when *The Greatest Expedition* of the Church began with the book of Acts, MMs like the Apostle Paul are prayed for and sent in order to glorify God and share the Gospel through marketplace connections.

In the Spring of 2018, I (Carrie) was introduced to this early desire for a movement by my pastor, Ken Nash, through a conversation centered on my service to the Board of Watermark Wesleyan Church. We mutually shared our leadership philosophies and connected in an equal desire to bring others to Jesus through our vocation. He helped me connect my faith, work, and my workplace team as "my congregation." Since Pastor Wayne shares the passion for this movement, I then had a fruitful conversation with him, too.

I was more than intrigued and expressed a desire to serve in any capacity that might be helpful. This resulted in an invitation to a national conference in June of 2019 where I had the opportunity to meet with leaders of The Wesleyan Church and other marketplace leaders. In this time together, I was bursting with excitement and a passion ignited to do more. I began to realize God's call to not only influence my workplace and region, but that I had the competence and willingness to have an even broader influence nationally. Ironically, in my vocation in recent years, I have worked diligently to establish an enterprise-wide strategy, rally a cohesive team, execute action with clear accountability, and then realize meaningful results. In the couple of months that followed, I was inspired by others to apply that same strategic approach to lead a Marketplace Multiplier strategic planning team comprised of diverse marketplace leaders from a variety of industries and skills across the U.S. We began to meet monthly to develop a strategy, action plan, and related accountabilities. The MM movement suddenly began to move!

The Purpose of Marketplace Multipliers

The movement of Marketplace Multipliers exists to equip all Christians to influence their workplace and integrate their faith by making disciples and unleashing the kingdom of God wherever they are. We believe there has never been a significant movement of God without the involvement of laity, moving disciple-making beyond the walls of the Church.

The Laity Have Left the Building!

"And Christ Himself gave some to be apostles, some to be prophets, some to be evangelists, and some to be shepherds and teachers, to prepare God's people for works of service, so that the body of Christ may be built up.

Ephesians 4:11-12

For a true movement to occur, laity need to be empowered and unleashed for ministry once again. While this is in the roots of both Wesleyan and United Methodists, the movement has all but come to a screeching halt. In his e-book, *Marks of Movement*,[1] Winfield Bevins describes this movement killer. When "movement killers" were introduced into Methodism in America that effectively hamstrung the movement. The first started in 1850, when the leaders of Methodism had tired of the Episcopalians and the Presbyterians who were deriding them as "uncouth and unlearned" ministers. They decided that all their circuit riders and local ministers had to complete four years of ordination studies in order to qualify. Growth ceased straightaway. As time marched on and the professionalization of clergy grew, laity became more and more removed from ministry resulting in the steady decline of the church.

---

[1] Winfield Bevins, *Marks of a Movement: What the Church Today Can Learn From the Wesleyan Revival,* Zondervan, 2019.

Bevins goes on to explain:

The main thing we can learn is that movements happen when they focus our energy on identifying, training, and empowering the next generation of leaders. Significant movements, such as the Wesleyan revival, are built on empowering non-ordained, lay leadership. Most people don't realize that John Wesley did more for lay ministry than any other major Christian leader in history since the time of the reformation. Until the 1700s, lay people could not serve in any type of ministry with a leadership position in the church. They were excluded from teaching, visiting the sick, or holding a leadership role in the church. Clergy were the only ones who had the authority to teach or preach in the church. As a result of Wesley's decision to begin using lay ministers in the Wesleyan revival, lay people today have an open door in most churches to share in ministry. In this regard, Wesley was a forerunner to the modern-day lay leader revolution in the church.(pg. 33-34).

Most churches are made up of about 1 percent clergy and 99 percent laity. By releasing and empowering laity for ministry, we are increasing our influence on the ground by 99%. We are suffering from two unique, but related issues.

First, there is the issue of "marginalization" of laity with denominations being clergy-centric in role and responsibility.

Second, there is an issue of the "minimization" of laity by under-utilizing the capacity of laity such as taking the offering and passing out bulletins. Congregations miss then the opportunity for laity to lead teams, spearhead initiatives and of course make disciples.

We believe this is a key reason why there has never been a significant, sustained movement of God without the full engagement of laity.

Marketplace Multipliers create the opportunity to empower and equip laity to do ministry (disciple and influence) as they go about their daily life in the workplace. As Marketplace Multipliers (MMs), we are intentional to integrate our faith and work to equip those around us in our workplaces, translating our influence into making disciples and multiplying the kingdom of God. We do this in whatever career or areas of influence we are led into. God is at work where we work, so we serve the higher interests of the kingdom while leading with excellence in the marketplace.

MM Based in Scripture

While the seeds of this particular expression of MM go back to 2017, we do not claim to have originated the foundational principles of integrating faith with work and stewarding our influence in the workplace. They are rooted in Scripture.

To *integrate* our faith with our work means we are to do our work...

> *...with sincerity of heart and reverence for the Lord. Whatever you do, work at it with all your heart, as working for the Lord, not for men, since you know that you will receive an inheritance from the Lord as a reward. It is the Lord Christ you are serving*
>
> **Colossians 3:22b-24**

It is the Lord whom we ultimately work for and whatever type of work it is can glorify God.

To *influence* others means to "mind your own business" by living your daily lives in a way that will "win the respect of outsiders" (I

Thessalonians 4:11-12).

Jesus equipped certain people to *prepare all people* to participate in His mission to go and make disciples so the Church flourishes:

> And Christ Himself gave some to be apostles, some to be prophets, some to be evangelists, and some to be shepherds and teachers, to prepare God's people for works of service, so that the body of Christ may be built up.
>
> **Ephesians 4:11-12**

Only God creates a movement, but we all have a role as the Spirit determines and empowers. This results in the engagement and mobilization of all God's people. More than a workforce, this is a "Kingdom Force" needed for the body of Christ to be built up.

In our lifetimes, MMs can be traced to the vision of people like Bill Bright and Loren Cunningham. In 1975, Bill (leading Campus Crusade for Christ) and Loren (leading Youth with A Mission) got together to consider the many areas of modern culture that still needed the Gospel. These individuals had already brought the gospel to millions around the world. But in their prayers, they believed the Lord showed them seven major areas of society, or "mountains" as they called them, which needed godly people to influence them, thereby influencing untold millions who were engaged in those seven mountains of society. They described these mountains of influence as business, government, media, arts and entertainment, education, family, and religion.

Opportunity for Influence

You have more influence than you think, mountains of influence in fact. This influence travels wherever you go. It is not restricted to where you worship. In fact, the vast majority of the influence of Christ in the world today is in marketplace settings, out in public, since the vast majority of Christians go to work every day around the globe. People often spend more time in the workplace than they spend at home. Imagine the eternal difference it makes as MMs begin to intentionally focus on integrating their faith and work, making disciples, and multiplying the kingdom in the marketplace.

You can do this. It is not for the super-Christians, the super-wealthy, or the super-gifted. Your marketplace influence can be used by God for good whether you work in business, health care, education, media, community service, the government or any other varieties of work. Even as you go about your life during retirement, doing volunteer work, or even during educational years, you are interacting with the marketplace and have influence.

Carrie's Story

My story (Carrie) began as I witnessed the culmination of leadership and faith at a very young age. My parents were highly engaged lay people in the Episcopal church (and both served as leaders in their vocation). My grandfather was a pastor in the Methodist church. I also witnessed the faith and fortitude required in raising my younger sister, Christine, with special needs.

For 20+ years of my healthcare career, I've had the privilege to apply my passion to make our healthcare system better for the benefit of those like my sister. Whether in a hospital, nursing and rehabilitation facility, or health insurance setting, this passion remains the same – to improve the quality of healthcare and to do so with an enthusiastic focus on excellence. This passion was ignited far before I was mature enough to recognize it. As I think about growing up with my younger sister physically challenged with cerebral palsy, I've personally witnessed the enormous trials, miraculous wins, and the opportunity to celebrate both. In 1992, my sister achieved the gold medal in the downhill slalom at the Lake Placid Special Olympics. She has since achieved a Master's in Special Education and was successful in having a family of her own – proof of God's resurrection power.

Christine brought a unique diversity to our family; she had special needs that often surpassed others' needs or desires. When we were in middle school, I vividly recall her desire to run with my friends and me in our backyard. I recall my personal struggle of whether to run ahead with my friends to be included or stay behind to be with her. As much as I feared I'd be perceived as slow and uninterested, my friends quickly recognized my sister needed me more at that moment. It was clear that others already appreciated her diversity – her disability was obvious to everyone – and the critical importance of her inclusion over my own. I learned at a young age that it doesn't matter what "outsiders" think; what matters are the people who need you to love and accept them for who they are in the moment they require it.

I'm fortunate to apply these life experiences and fuel my passion in an organization that has empowered me to engage others in a quest to improve the quality of healthcare across 1.5 million people and in 39 upstate New York counties. I'm now privileged to serve many on my team, encourage diversity and inclusion, influence cross-functional collaboration, and execute results to improve health. It is through my life experience that I passionately seek to put others' needs ahead of my own. This is so relevant in the healthcare arena where there is always something to improve; there is always a patient needing physical/ emotional support and healing; there is always an opportunity to pour into front-line employees and disciple them as we work together in the quality improvement journey. I firmly believe this is the way Jesus would function if He were on Earth today – discipling as we work alongside others. In fact, when Jesus was discipling the disciples, most of that ministry was done outside the Temple. Jesus literally walked alongside people, dined with family and friends, had conversations with the tax collector, and joined in community festivities. Jesus modeled marketplace multipliers for us over 2,000 years ago!

As Pastor Ken helped me truly see the connection of my vocation to the opportunity to influence others in their faith, I have been unleashed to equip and empower Christians to integrate their faith in the workplace, not compartmentalize it. As I have begun to do this, I strive to meet people where they are in every interaction. I fully appreciate the importance of inclusion, humility, and kindness. I'm willing to expose my own vulnerability to connect with others. I've specifically experienced vocational conversations evolve to faith conversations amidst the need to overcome challenges in the workplace. By openly communicating, trusting one another, and expressing deep-hearted desires for change, we are capable of finding strength in Jesus together. Our titles are "checked at the door," and we build each other up to courageously tackle what God has called us to change.

Fundamentally, it comes down to building lasting relationships. This means connecting with people who work for me, those who work across from me as peers, and those who are higher than me in an organization. These relationships become true equal partnerships as I seek to know them deeply, understand their wiring, what drives them, and share the same about myself in the process. In the most fruitful of relationships, our faith exudes and we partner together in new ways, find new strength, and support one another in bold ways by pouring into each other when needed most.

It's not uncommon for me to be asked, "Where does your energy come from?" or "What fuels you?" The simple answer is my unwavering faith in Jesus Christ. I want to give all the accolades to God as I seek to live my life focused on Philippians 4:13:

> *I can do all things through Christ who strengthens me.*

Wayne's Story

My (Wayne) personal passion for ministry in the marketplace is deeply personal. It arises out of biblical and theological convictions, but it has been imprinted on me through two very significant longer-term relationships.

The first is with my dad, after whom I am named – Wayne Keith Schmidt. He was very much a work-with-his-hands craftsman and small business owner. I began working in our family business when I was 12 years old, sweeping floors and pounding nails. I worked with my dad after school and in the summers – when times were good, our primary work was trim carpentry. When times were a bit challenging, we also did framing, which was labeled "rough construction." When times were really tough, we did remodeling – which my dad described as "taking twice as long and costing twice as much" as he estimated.

My dad was first and foremost a craftsman – he built custom cabinets in a time when prefabricated cupboards were not known for quality. He might be described as "blue collar" – his filing system was often located on the dashboard of his truck covered with a bit of sawdust.

As a teenager, I was deeply impressed by

two things. The first is that my dad was the same man at church as he was at home as he was at work. The fruit of the Spirit was evident in him in all of those contexts – he was consistent in living what he believed. The second was the influence he had with others in the residential construction trade – many of whom would not likely begin their spiritual journeys by walking into a local church, but rather would be impressed by integrity of character and excellent work in the marketplace. My dad quietly but winsomely not only lived his faith, he let coworkers know he was not who he was simply because he was a good person, but because of Jesus.

I saw the potential of ministry in the marketplace as modeled by my father. Perhaps that combined with an entrepreneurial spirit caused me to dream of building our family construction business into a development company. While I never would be the capable perfectionist that made my dad such a respected craftsman, I was wired to build things in another way and entered college as a business major. While ultimately God redirected my work with a call to vocational ministry, to this day I'm energized by the Kingdom impact of marketplace multipliers.

The second relationship that greatly influenced my conviction of marketplace multiplication is my accountability partner, Paul Anthes. Beginning in 1985, we've met every other week to "spur one another on to love and good deeds." Other than my wife Jan, no one knows me better than Paul. In encouraging each other to be faithful in little things that add up to a life that honors God, we've also asked each other how we are doing in the private world of our souls.

Paul founded and owns a wealth management firm. His everyday work would be described as "white collar." He is as called to his work as I am to mine. Helping clients make long-term financial decisions opens up a variety of conversations about what is important to them, what they want their legacy to be, how much is enough, and the potential for generosity. In his work he is making disciples, but as Jesus said a person can't serve both God and money. Where their treasure is, that's where their hearts will be (Matthew 6:19-24).

Paul is involved in his local church, in coaching other leaders for true success in the workplace, and in the governance of a university and various parachurch organizations. But he is very clear, and in fact has assigned a descriptor to it – these are his Non-Vocational Ministry Activities (NVMA). His wife Cindie, the COO of his firm Loran, and myself serve as Paul's NVMA advisors as he considers more opportunities than his schedule permits him to invest in. But he has attached this NVMA label to these activities because he wants to be clear that his ministry is not only what he does at church or for parachurch organizations, but what he does every day in his Vocational Ministry Activities – his workplace is a place of ministry, of making disciples.

Paul is as intense about the integrity of his character and the integration of his faith with his work as I am. He is "called to ministry" in a variety of contexts, and the context beyond his family where he invests most of his time in his business.

Cumulatively, for over 50 years I've been influenced by these two MMs. Because of them and so many others I am more passionate than ever for the potential of every person, whether their work is characterized as "white collar" or "blue collar," to make disciples as they integrate their faith with their work and steward their influence.

Kay's Story

As a lay person who has worked in the corporate world and launched multiple businesses before answering my call to unique ministry, I grow ever more passionate every year to be a part of a movement that wakes us Christians to once again live our life as

a disciple and introduce Jesus to others. It
is though churches and their congregations
have been in an ever-deepening slumber. So
many churches have forgotten their purpose
of making disciples and have instead become
country clubs of sorts serving its members
with privileges and benefits rather than
being a movement in their local mission field
serving, loving neighbors, sharing the Good
News, and growing in discipleship as they
disciple others.

In conducting countless church
consultations for revitalization and training
and coaching thousands of laity and clergy
across the country, I have experienced a
stuckness: apathy, and lack of capacity for
living out the mission we are called to fulfill.
I don't offer this as a statement of criticism;
it is simply the reality. It is sometimes
easier to launch something new then it is to
transform something existing. While I still
have hope for the local church and continue
to invest heavily in working with them for

revitalization, deploying people out of the church is the future (and frankly has been our past). We were never about becoming settlers, we were always intended to be pioneers continuously moving to build relationships, serve, and share Christ. MM is a movement that empowers laity to live out vocational and ministry calls simultaneously. There has been a developing compartmentalization of vocation and ministry over the past several decades. MM allows us to reverse this trend and instead live a holistic life where one is a Christ-follower 24/7, even when at work!

The other reason I believe in MM is because it takes the focus away from being building and congregational-centered. In the past when culture was church-centric, congregations met new people at the worship door to receive them. Culture was "sending" people to church. But in today's culture, the church is counter cultural. People are not showing up on the church doorstep to be received. Depending on which study you read, most mission fields are more than 70 percent unchurched. Just like other growing movements such as missional communities, home (micro) churches and faith-based social innovations, MM is returning the mission of disciple-making back to the streets where it originated with Jesus! People will be much more open and trusting in hearing the Good News from a trusted friend or co-worker than they are from the church.

Let me share one final reason for my passion around MM. Sometimes the local church, its judicatory leadership, and/or its denominational structure has gotten so complicated, complex, antiquated, and inflexible that reaching people through these traditional means is becoming more and more difficult. Clergy-dependent congregations, laity feeling dis-empowered, and the enormous overhead expenses to be a traditional church in a huge facility with high salaries further complicates the congregation's ability to be vital and effective. MM is an organic, relationally-driven movement that has virtually no cost that has a higher probability in reaching new people using the largest segment of the body of Christ, the laity!

CHAPTER THREE

Launching a Marketplace Multipliers Movement

As a Marketplace Multiplier, I (Carrie) have a deep appreciation for the key role of pastors in identifying and recruiting MM leaders. Feel free to listen in on a conversation with Carrie and Pastor Ken Nash as they discuss this very topic on a podcast at:

https://msb.press/multiply

Pastor Ken Nash, while serving at Watermark Wesleyan Church in Hamburg, New York opened my (Carrie's) eyes to the influence I have in the workplace. This was not the typical influence we tend to think about for all leaders in the marketplace, but this was about evangelical influence. Given my leadership role and the trusting relationships

I have established with so many in my workplace, I was awakened to the fact that I can be even more intentional in influencing lives for Christ – every day of the week. He provided meaningful prayer, encouragement, empowerment, and connected me with others, namely Wayne, to advance the movement. I was energized to put this into action!

This pastor/marketplace multiplier partnership is vital to aligning what occurs inside the walls of church and outside the church walls in the marketplace. There is a key role pastors can play in this movement. Here are a few examples of ways we encourage pastors to adopt to create a marketplace multiplier culture in the local church:

- Create the awareness for marketplace leaders to "see" the opportunity to unleash God's kingdom and create a multiplying movement

- Partner, encourage, and empower the MM to be used by God by launching or joining the MM movement in their local church or region

- Send/commission the MM as part of a worship experience

- Pray for the MMs continued awareness, action, and fortitude to integrate faith and make disciples

- Share your MM experiences with other pastors to fuel the movement

- Seek out additional MMs

Pastor Ken and I launched a Marketplace Multiplier movement that goes beyond Watermark Wesleyan Church and seeks to engage all Wesleyan churches and their marketplace multipliers in Western New York (WNY). This larger movement of marketplace multipliers has now been structured into what we call "chapters" (groups of MMs in a local church) and could easily become ecumenical and/or be used to start a similar movement in other denominations.[2] The WNY MM Chapter is early in its formation with a desire to:

- Gather WNY business leaders across local Wesleyan churches who influence their workplace

---

[2] For information on the Methodist Marketplace Multipliers Movement, visit MarketplaceMultipliers.com

- Support, inspire, and equip WNY business leaders with meaningful insights through educational content, regular dialogue, shared experiences, and action to integrate faith

- Help increase intentionality in the workplace to integrate faith with work and make disciples

We've intentionally identified key values of a Marketplace Multiplier Chapter that will stay centered on:

- Heart – Emotional intelligence, vulnerability, inspiration, Spirit-filled guidance

- Head – Wisdom/discernment, focus, intentionality

- Support – Dialogue, inspiration, shared testimonies, networking

- Resources – Equipping content

- Connection to other MMs

- Challenge & Accountability – Bias for action, driven to calling, commitment to disciple, Kingdom focus, and gospel saturation

The deep respect I have for my pastor is not an exception among MMs; it is the norm. Dave Gerry is a MM who has made such an impact as a Kingdom multiplier. He shares some wise words yet blunt words concerning the deep, mutually respectful partnership between pastors and MMs. He says, "People who claim to be MMs but just want to do their own thing, being accountable to no one and having nothing but criticism for the local church, aren't truly MMs – they're mavericks. MMs deep down want the blessing of their pastor and their church. Sure, they experience times of frustration and wish certain things would change in their local church. But they want to be commissioned, to be sent into the marketplace – to sense that what they do every day is an extension of their local church and in partnership with their pastor."

Pastors in congregations large and small, in communities of various sizes and demographics, are catching the vision of being a sending church. (A sending church is described as a congregation who values and empowers laity to be discipling disciples in their everyday lives and workplaces.) Just as the Apostle Paul was prayed over and sent by the Church on his missionary journeys, pastors are casting the vision for and praying over those who journey into the marketplace every day. Many pastors are sharing a message or a series of messages on the value of work and its Kingdom potential. Some pastors are sharing their series with a MM giving one of the messages, or highlighting the ministries of MMs each week of the series. Many also conclude a message or series by praying over those who are sensing a call to the marketplace and welcoming them to participate in their local church MM chapter.

Bryan Savage is the Lead Pastor of Greenville Community Church located Greenville, MI. They launched the Marketplace Multiplier vision in their church through a dialogue between two guests – one ordained and the other a MM. This was followed by an opportunity for people to be prayed for as they seek to represent Christ in their own workplaces. Pastor Bryan then launched a series of messages on a biblical view of work and witness. The first sermon was delivered by him to affirm and clarify the MM vision specifically for their church and context. The next couple of messages came from laity representing a marketplace perspective. Through this process the core group of their MM chapter was raised up, empowered, commissioned, and sent to minister and multiply in the marketplace.

Katie Lance is the Lead Pastor of Thrive Church located Eaton Rapids, MI. She began the MM movement in her church by personally recruiting MM, Steve Laginess, to partner with her in the founding of their local church chapter. Her invitation and his commitment took place a few months in advance of them "going public" with their congregation about the launch of their local church MM chapter. Steve was baptized just a year before engaging in MM leadership and has a powerful story of life transformation through his full surrender to God which he readily shares with others. He exudes the Spirit of Hope as he helps others dig deep spiritually and receive freedom. Steve works in a machine shop. There are people he has known for 30 years in his shop who see the difference in his life and he gets to share more about the reason for this difference.

In addition to whatever general invitation is given for MM, the pastor's selection of a MM partner to host/lead the local church's MM movement/chapter is important. It should be a matter of prayer and discernment to identify and list a few potential partners. That partner may be someone the pastor knows well, perhaps even discipled – or it may be someone they don't know well but respect for how they already practice integrating their faith with their work and steward their influence. It might be someone who hasn't been involved in other roles in the church because of their travel or work schedules, but may be able to make a focused contribution by partnering in convening the other MMs to gather together for equipping, connection and encouragement (i.e. chapter meetings). This MM leader would be a person who multiplies leaders as well as disciples.

Ideally, the pastor and MM partner models a healthy relationship between clergy and laity. At its best it becomes an "Ezra and Nehemiah Kingdom Partnership." At a significant and historical time in the life of the people of God in the Old Testament, Ezra the priest (pastor and teacher) and Nehemiah (a lay person working in government) combine their unique contributions through partnership (Nehemiah 8:9-10 and 12:26, 36). Ezra was to give leadership to a spiritual revival and reform – a rejection of the practices that had been adopted from other nations and a return to the truth. Nehemiah was moved to give leadership to an economic and political reform, creating a stable and sustainable context in which the spiritual revival could flourish. They were equally devout and called, but to different realms of Kingdom work. Neither would have experienced the "joy of the Lord as their strength" without the other.

Ezra and Nehemiah were originally one book, not two. They were not separated until the time of Origen in the 3rd century B.C. Perhaps the fact that they were originally together and then separated is symbolically significant. We don't know all the reasons for the separation into two books, but there has been speculation about possible motivations. Perhaps one reason for the separation is Ezra was considered more "sacred" and Nehemiah's work more "secular." But together they accomplished something that led to a revival as well as a renewal of the city. Rebuilding the temple without rebuilding the community was not enough. They were partners in ministry. Both were uniquely gifted for the ministry God was calling them individually and in partnership with one another.

While it often is the pastor who identifies and recruits MM leadership, that is not the only way it works. Sometimes the partnership between MM and pastor begins with the MM. For instance, Julie Richardson is a pharmacist who also owns an insurance business. She grew up in the community where she lives and the church she attends. She is widely known in the business community, in the schools and in local government. She is a MM in every sense of the word and is so grateful for her pastor, Peter Damaska. She has been energized by the MM initiative and invited her pastor to consider a chapter in their local church. They now are ministry partners along with the Discipleship Pastor Sarah Damaska in founding and leading their MM chapter.

CHAPTER FOUR

The Ministry of a Marketplace Multiplier

Integrating Faith with Work

It's hard to take someone on a journey you've never been on. It's hard to be a guide in an area you've not visited before. A phrase that is stuck with me related this states that "You cannot impart what you do not possess." Because of this truth, our own spiritual growth and maturity is linked to our ability to minister in the marketplace setting that God has placed us. It doesn't mean that a lack of maturity should prevent us from integrating our faith, but as we grow and mature our influence will increase.

There needs to be congruence and consistency between what the Bible teaches and how we act and operate in the marketplace. Major gaps here could be viewed as hypocrisy and limit our reach and influence. Pre-Christians often have knowledge or awareness of what the Bible says and use this knowledge, whether accurate or not, to evaluate Christians they work with.

So many of the attributes we are called to in the Bible make us relevant and attractive to those around us. Think in terms of love, mercy, grace, compassion, forgiveness, honesty, and others. People are wired to be attracted to authentic expressions of these attributes. Through these we earn the right to build relationships and even gain the respect of some of the people we work with.

As part of our Christian beliefs, there are several key beliefs that relate directly to integrating our faith in our work. These beliefs are a "subset" or part of a biblical worldview and not something that is added. This is a natural outcome of complete surrender to the Lordship of Jesus Christ.

- God owns it all! (Psalm 24: 1-2).

- Everything we have is a gift from God. As Ken Boa has said, "We brought nothing to the party." This truth leads to total life stewardship.

- We have been bought at a price – so our life is not our own (1 Corinthians 6:19-20).

- Jesus is Lord over every area of our lives. There is no exclusion.

- There is no sacred and secular. Everything is sacred or spiritual, and everything matters.

- The Bible teaches that our faith should be integrated with every area of life including our vocation. As "integrators," living out our faith in and through our work is success.

- All Christ followers are ministers – a priesthood of all believers. We can consider those God has placed in our work world as our congregation (1 Peter 2:9).

- Be prepared to give an answer followed by "good behavior" (1 Peter 3:1).

- We are to shine like stars as we behave like Christians in the marketplace (Philippians 2: 14-16).

- All believers are "sent" and have a "calling." For marketplace people, integration of faith in and through our work is pleasing to God.

- Believers in the marketplace are a Kingdom Force and it is needed. We can reach and influence people that might not ever make it to church.

A Quote from Os Guinness, "One audience, an audience of one," illustrates a way to approach life and determine who we will choose to try and please. It seems that we are wired in a manner that leads us to try and please someone. It seems like a part of our human nature by default. However, we have the choice of who that someone will be. It could be friends, coworkers, our boss, relatives, and others in our lives. Or, it could be that God is at the top of that list and He is the one we focus on pleasing first and foremost, and above all else. Putting God first is the only way that things will make sense in life. Trying to please others and find fulfillment from pleasing them may provide some temporary satisfaction and enjoyment, but it will eventually come up empty. It is by putting God first that we understand how to love and serve others.

As we consider our attitude about life, once again Jesus modeled this for us. An application of this concept is the call to be a servant just as Jesus was. This is true for everyone and especially for those in leadership. Consider what Matthew 20:28 says: "Just as the Son of Man did not come to be served, but to serve, and give his life as a ransom for many." This is a strong statement about how Christians should lead. Jesus modeled it for us through his life and ministry.

Intentionality Combined with what Happens Naturally

It might be easy to approach work with a compartmentalized mindset. Yes, we want to be honest and trustworthy and demonstrate other attributes of a Christian. But we don't see the tremendous opportunities that exist around us in our everyday work. Ministry is at church or other ministries in my community. Work is about doing my job and earning a living to provide for me and my family. It seems that when we develop the belief and mindset that our work is ministry, we are often opened up to see numerous opportunities to live out our faith in our vocation and work settings. As we practice this more and more, it becomes natural to respond in a way that's consistent with our Christian beliefs at work. It's not forced or seen as just an event, but rather as a consistent lifestyle related to our work.

As we shift our mindset that our work is our ministry, we can change the perspective from this being an obligation or duty to see it more as an opportunity and a privilege. Experiencing the joy of ministering to others that God has placed in our lives becomes something we naturally desire. This type of experience can become a natural source of motivation to see our vocation both as work and ministry combined in healthy ways.

When we are paying attention, the marketplace offers multiple opportunities to implement our faith in day-to-day activities and decisions that are made. We don't need to be preachy in these activities, but we can reveal the reasons and why we do what we do, and why we choose not to do other things. Our actions can naturally reveal our morals, standards, and conduct.

Be a Generous Listener

Real listening is hard work! To suspend our current thoughts and ideas to give our full focus to what the other person is saying is a great gift that we can give. Who doesn't want to be listened to and understood? All of us desire that at times in our lives.

So, what's the motive? Am I just listening to be polite until I get a chance to speak? Am I using my mental energy to arrange my comments to argue or impress once I get to speak? This is so easy to do; it takes no effort at all.

Placing a higher value on what the other

person has to say than what I am thinking is an effective strategy. Humility plays an important part here. What makes me think that what I have to say is more important than what the other person has to say? The call to love and serve others fits well with this concept of honoring others above ourselves (Phil 2:3-4).

It can be helpful to consider what your desired results are from a conversation. Is it to be heard, or is it to truly understand the other person as best as you can? Taking the attitude of a servant can allow us to focus on listening to understand the other person.

Remember Prevenient Grace

God is already working; we're joining with God. The fact is, we can't save anyone. Only God can do that. Having this truth available can free us to focus on "our part" and trust God for "God part." We have heard it said that we should look where God is at work and join God. This can be an effective strategy in the marketplace.

Success can be defined as doing our part well and trusting God for the outcomes God wants to produce. This lifts the burden of being responsible for results that are beyond our control. While we hope and pray for progress in the lives of other people, we are not in control of that.

Dealing with Skepticism

From time to time, you may encounter some skepticism or maybe even a push back of people believing you can't share your faith in the workplace. We are reminded, "Preach the Gospel at all times. When necessary, use words," per St. Francis of Assisi. Add to this the fact that there are times when actions speak louder than words. There is great freedom in how we conduct ourselves and in the messages that our actions send.

There are settings where it's more difficult to share faith in the workplace than others. There is no doubt about this. However, we know of no rules against being kind, compassionate, honest, trustworthy, forgiving, supportive, and other attributes that should be a normal part of the Christian's life.

So, even if one is unable to use words, there are still tremendous opportunities to be a witness in the marketplace. For many, this creates irresistible curiosity about why a person would conduct themselves this way in all settings. This may well open the door for sharing more in appropriate ways.

There are also more freedoms to bring our faith to the workplace than we often realize. Becoming informed about what is legally allowed can be helpful and encouraging. But you also want to be aware of the environment and its expectations. You could be legally in the right and still lose the ability to interact with and influence others by acting inappropriately in the given environment.

Putting the Pieces Together

What does this ministry in the workplace look like practically? For starters, we need to realize that every workplace is different and each MM is on their own unique discipleship journey. Couple that with the uniqueness of every person you encounter in the marketplace and we begin to see there is no one tried and true, step-by-step approach. I (Kay) often ask people who attend a workshop how long they dated their significant other before making a commitment to marriage. As you can imagine, there is a vast range of answers from two weeks to years and years. How can this be?

Each relationship is unique. It's different. There are no rules in developing these relationships. Each one matures at its own pace. This is no different than the development of ministry for a MM. Given this understanding, let's explore a general idea of what ministry might entail as a MM.

Prayer

As with anything, your ministry in the marketplace begins and ends with prayer.

Bathe all you do and say in prayer. Ask God to reveal to you who is ready to reach out to, who needs a kind word, how to model your faith, who needs to be encouraged, what words to offer, etc. Pray for clarity and confirmation. Pray to have the eyes and ears to see and hear what God desires for you to hear as you show up to serve in your marketplace.

It Starts with Relationship Building

Before we can influence or disciple, we must first invest in relationships. This means investing in people out of your desire to know them, know their story, what they are celebrating, what pains they are carrying, what wounds need healing, what is going on in their lives, etc. We invest in people to do life with people. When you interact with people in your workplace for up to forty hours or more every week, you are honored with the opportunity to do life with them. We just have to be intentional about authentically investing, connecting, and relating as we model Christian values and relationships. We will never be privileged to hear a person's story until they trust us and know we care about them as a person.

Demonstrating the fact that you care about someone on a standalone basis is a powerful force. This is consistent with what Scripture would encourage us to do. We need to try and see the value that God sees in every human being. "People don't care how much you know until they know about how much you care." This truth applies to forming a relationship with someone before you even share your faith or testimony with them. Demonstrate that you see intrinsic value in them.

Their Story

As the relationship builds over time (at its own unique pace with each individual), there will come a time when you as the MM will have the opportunity to ask a deeper question or reveal something about yourself that takes the conversation and the relationship to a different level. When this occurs, there is a new knowing in the relationship of one or both of you. It grows and deepens the relationship. This is likely when the MM can begin to share tidbits of their faith or perhaps even their faith story. In the sharing, curiosity is heightened giving the MM more and more opportunity over time to share. It is also a time for the MM to offer probing questions to help the person reflect, consider, reconsider, wander, wonder, etc. It is a time of searching and some general soul searching.

It is important for the MM to know that s/he is not responsible for creating a lightning-bolt reaction, a soul shift, or even a reconsideration. It is our responsibility as a MM to be obedient when God asks us to show up. It could be a question we are prompted to ask or a story we feel called to share. God uses us right where we are, right how we are, and with the right words on our tongue. Show up, be obedient, and then watch the Holy Spirit do the work and the heavy lifting.

Walk Alongside

After you begin to see a growing curiosity or even a tiny advancement in their faith walk, this is your time to walk alongside them at their pace in their own timing. This is the time of being in the support role – ever encouraging yet not pushing. This might be a time when you can begin to pray with them. Be gentle. Ask them how you can help or how you can assist them with their next step.

Discipleship

When the time is right, you will know it or they might even ask for it. When their curiosity is turned up high, they will be hungry. They will have questions, desire resources, want more and deeper conversations, etc. This is when the relationship turns to you as a disciple becoming a disciple-maker. This is where you begin to help this person on their discipleship journey. And this is when it is great to lean on the resources of your own church. What is the discipleship pathway your church uses with the congregation? Use the same pathway and the same resources as you disciple this person in your marketplace.

This may happen at lunch, on breaks, before work, after work, etc. This may be a one-on-one experience or it may turn into a small group. Once discipleship begins, you will likely have others watching who will eventually ask questions and possibly even want to join in. Yes, it is another movement in action.

Additional Resources

Here are some resources that you might find to be helpful to reinforce evangelism and discipleship:

Get Their Name by Kay Kotan and Bishop Bob Farr – This book explores how to build relationships with the unchurched and walk through a natural process that leads from a first conversation to the discipleship pathway.

Reveal: Where Are You? by Greg Hawkins and Cally Parkinson – This book reveals the four spiritual movements of exploring Christ, growing in Christ, Close to Christ, and Christ Centered.

Follow Me – What's Next for You? by Greg Hawkins and Cally Parkinson – This resource identifies the four categories of spiritual catalysts:

1. Spiritual beliefs and attitudes,

2. Organized church activities

3. Personal spiritual practices, such as prayer and reflecting on Scripture

4. Spiritual activities with others – happening largely outside the church, spiritual friendships, evangelism, serving.

Stride: Creating a Discipleship Pathway for Your Church by Mike Schreiner & Ken Willard – This book outlines the need for an intentional faith development process and how to create one.

Discipleship in the New Expedition by Phil Maynard[3] – From the Essentials Track of *The*

Greatest Expedition, this resource explores all the elements of discipleship and how to lead someone in their discipleship journey to become a disciple maker.

Your Spiritual Journey: A Personal Guide by Gary Rohrmayer.[4] You are involved in a disciple-making all the way from respectfully planting seeds in the earliest of stages leading to a faith commitment all the way to maturity in Christian faith. Stages of Discipleship:

- Not interested – resisting
- Curiously searching – questioning
- Searching assertively – responding
- Faith commitment – embracing
- Experiencing new life – adjusting
- Is growing in community – stabilizing
- Living missionally – reproducing
- Engel Scale[5] – Having an understanding where

---

[4] www.yourjourneyresource.com

[5] https://irp-cdn.multiscreensite.com/2988a589/files/uploaded/the-engel-scale.pdf

one is the Engel Scale and developing the ability to estimate where others are on this scale offers great benefits. Being aware that there is a natural progression for most people in the journey toward accepting Christ, can help us be better in tune with where they are and how we can help them move forward.

- Organic Outreach for Ordinary People [6] may help you shape a personal approach to passing on the good news of Jesus in natural ways. This is not a system or a program. It's a collection of biblical practices that you can incorporate into your life starting today. You can begin right where God has placed you.

Gary Rohrmayer has more recently written *Spiritual Conversations – Creating and Sustaining Them Without Being a Jerk*. This is an approach to evangelism and discipleship that encourages a "coaching" approach as you come alongside another.

Permission Evangelism by Michael Simpson. A practical resource to address the common Christian fear of personal evangelism – you have to be forceful or corner people. Rather,

---

[6] https://www.organicoutreach.org

sharing is most effective and best received when it is conducted in a manner that is respectful of the unbeliever and aimed at securing the unbeliever's willing acquiescence to hearing the Gospel.

CHAPTER FIVE

Co-Vocational Marketplace Multipliers, Pastors, and Churches

In this low-touch, high-tech world, people are craving relationships and community. This has only intensified in our post-pandemic world. The MM movement is so highly relational and exactly how Jesus modeled it for us. That being the case, there is another potential layer to the MM movement for your consideration.

Most of us are familiar with the term bi-vocational pastor. This is likely a pastor who is working a secular job to "pay the bills" while s/he pastors a small church. The intention is for the church to grow to the size that it can eventually support the pastor full time. The secular job is a means to the end. Consider instead a co-vocational pastor. A co-vocational pastor is a person (could be lay or clergy) who intentionally straddles the church ministry role and the secular job role and is considered permanent – not temporary or a stepping stone. A huge advantage of co-vocational pastors is the natural spheres of influence and disciple-making in their employment beyond the walls of the church and in the marketplace. An example of this co-vocational role can be found among our MMs is Pete Benson who is featured on one of our initial MM podcasts. He is an ordained Wesleyan minister involved in a non-denominational church in Nashville (Church of the City). After being a local church pastor and church planter he co-founded Beacon Capital Management.[7] His work in providing financial advice naturally leads to spiritual conversations (long term goals, what's important to you, what is your legacy, etc.) and disciple-making opportunities (where your treasure is…you can't serve God and money). He funded and participates in the Benson School of Business at Southern Wesleyan University, which has

---

[7] https://beaconcm.com

structured a dual major so ministry students can also have a business degree (by the way, at SWU many major can also dual major with a ministry degree).

Not only are individuals pursuing a co-vocational ministry, but increasingly whole churches are adopting a co-vocational approach. In addition to receiving donations they are initiating non-profit and for-profit ministry initiatives that create additional streams of income as well as connecting them to people in marketplace contexts in a whole new way.

Previous generations were co-vocational mainly out of economic necessity, but the emerging generation seems to be more interested in co-vocational as a ministry strategy and a lifestyle.

As mentioned previously, Priscilla & Aquila were business owners which uniquely positioned them to share their faith in the marketplace. Did they have the same "freedom" Paul defended as an apostle (I Corinthians 9:15-18)? Intentionally co-vocational (NAE conversation, churches being co-vocational)? This must have added to Paul's delight in working with Aquila and Priscilla in the same business, and at times he supported himself in this way (Acts 20:34; 1 Thessalonians 2:9; 2 Thessalonians 3:8).

When not preaching and teaching we can imagine Paul, Aquila, and Priscilla working together in a shop with canvas and leather. They were not ashamed of their "secular careers." We can envision them taking pride in their "blue collar" work. They were in the tent business first of all for the glory of God. Incidentally, it just also happened to put bread on their table, too.

My wife, Jan, and I (Wayne) visited Corinth on a cruise and toured the ruins of "main street." Their tent business would have placed them strategically right in the heart of the community: doing life and ministry right there where all the action is taking place, day in and day out.

Wayne's son, Jordan, is a MM who

manages a warehouse and spiritually invests in his employees. The office supply distributor he works for, Integrity, is owned by a MM. While there are challenges, Jordan is grateful for work for an employer who seeks to live up to their name "Integrity" and where he is encouraged to grow personally and spiritually.

CHAPTER SIX

Creating a Local Church Marketplace Multiplier Movement

To create a local church MM movement, you will want to gather as a "chapter" that functions as an incubator and base camp for marketplace multiplication. The chapter is not an end in itself. Instead, a chapter (or whatever you might call such a movement in your local context and expedition) is a base camp and incubator for identifying, equipping, commissioning, and sending MMs into the marketplace.

What makes a person a marketplace multiplier is not attending a MM meeting at church. Yet, at the same time the ministry of the MM is grounded in and encouraged by the local church. The chapter, like an incubator, provides a safe place of growth in the capacity to integrate faith with work and steward the influence of excellence in work in order to contribute to the spiritual growth of others. Like the Expedition Team's Base Camp, it is a place to be refreshed and resourced in order to elevate the level of impact of the MM in his or her workplace.

The MM chapter is convened quarterly by the pastor and a MM partner. Why quarterly? We believe this is often enough for the peer encouragement needed and provided by MMs. This frequency doesn't consume the calendar of the MM so that they don't have the needed time to invest in workplace relationships and disciple making. It also allows the MM to participate in other small group and discipleship activities in their local church, preventing MMs from becoming siloed from others in the congregation. It additionally leaves room for periodic equipping activities that might be provided for the marketplace multiplication. It is important for MMs to still have the bandwidth to continuously grow and mature in their own discipleship journey.

So, the chapter, as the basic building block, provides a rhythm of peer encouragement that is relational and regular. It is relational because the chapter meetings are an opportunity for MMs to encourage one another, learn from each other and pray for each other. These regular quarterly meetings provide a reminder to each participant to integrate their faith with their work and steward their influence.

A chapter should be contextualized in each local church and community. It is a place to live out the biblical challenge:

> *And let us consider how we may spur one another on toward love and good deeds, not giving up meeting together, as some are in the habit of doing, but encouraging one another.*
>
> **Hebrews 10:24-25**

This encouragement focuses on the two core commitments of integrating faith with work and stewarding influence in order to make disciples. So, while the "agenda" for the meeting varies from church to church, the heart of the meeting remains the same wherever in the world MMs are gathering.

As the MM movement gains momentum, churches are creatively shaping the chapter meetings in order to best catalyze marketplace multiplication in their context. So many historical, cultural and geographical factors may have a formative impact. Most find it is best to start simple and then further adapt the agenda of the chapter as they learn from each quarterly meeting. The gathering of the MMs is less about having a "meeting" and much more about encouragement, support, and equipping.

When the broader MM movement was just emerging, "contextualization conversations" began not only in North America, but around the world. Leaders in the Asia-Pacific arena wrestled with how MM chapters in India or Bangladesh might differ, and in turn recognized they may have more in common than they would have with chapters in Singapore or Australia. At the same time, these conversations were initiated among Spanish-language chapters in North America and through Iberoamerica, where national language and cultural differences exist.

The MM movement is essentially local – rooted in a church and in a community. It is simultaneously global – spreading to "the ends of the earth." Years ago, the term "glocal" was coined – global and local – and this aptly describes the emerging MM movement. Local "chapters" may have occasion to gather with other chapters from a larger state or regional area for deeper connection, learning and encouragement.

The chapters all have a common purpose – to encourage and equip MMs to live and share their faith in their workplaces. Some chapters have a focus that extends this common purpose in a unique way. For instance, some local churches equip MMs to convene and lead workplace groups. They meet before, during a lunch hour or after the work day, in person or through technology. They meet to study the Bible, to pray, or to help those exploring spiritually to find answers to their questions. These are not "holy huddles" or "exclusive enclaves" of holier-than-thou Christians, but those seeking to share Good News with others or help them to deepen their discipleship in Christ.

Other chapters may have a cause. There are groups that seek to meet a specific community need or engage in more comprehensive community development. They find serving to be a way people in all places in their faith journey can join together to make a difference in their city or town.

Some churches see the potential in some MMs to create missional communities of their church or to plant other churches. These MMs are an extension of their church as it seeks to permeate its geographical area with the Gospel.

So, the chapters are built on core commitments, but can be creative in ways that fulfill the church's vision and meet

the needs in the community. Pastor Dawn
Damon leads Tribes' Church, a multi-ethnic
congregation with a heart for its cities and
a core of MMs who are gifted entrepreneurs
and well connected with both businesses and
nonprofits in the greater Grand Rapids, MI
region area. It is leveraging those strengths to
equip people to start businesses in a variety
of contexts, bringing vitality to multi-ethnic
and multi-economic communities and in
the process creating new marketplaces for
disciple-making.

CHAPTER SEVEN

Steps to Launch a Marketplace Multiplier Movement Chapter

The mission of your local church MM chapter is a "learning and launching" gathering for Christians seeking to integrate their faith with their work and steward their influence in the marketplace in order to make disciples. It is to encourage one another and equip each person through shared learning experiences.

Following are the recommended steps for starting a chapter in your local congregation, district, and/or community:

STEP 1 – Register Your Local Church Chapter

Tell us of your existing local gathering of marketplace multipliers or your intent to launch one as a hub in your area by providing the information listed below. This is the best way to stay connected to others doing what you're doing or what you hope to do. Visit **MarketplaceMultipliers.com**[8] and register your intent to start a chapter. This will connect you to useful tools, stories from other chapters, and inspiring ideas you can implement in your context.

You don't need to know everything about your chapter to register it. Registering is simply a starting point to connect with other MM Movements and provide information and resources to help you get started and thrive.

Chapter Registration:

When a chapter registers, it includes a place for the Lead Pastor & MM info (reinforcing partnership), church name and location, and a menu with options for *My local chapter…*

---

[8] Wesleyan Church groups visit msb.press/wesleyan

- ❑ has been meeting regularly for some time... we're all in!

- ❑ just started and had our first meetings... we're rolling!

- ❑ is starting soon and has a date on the calendar...we're excited!

- ❑ is forming but not official yet...we're dreaming!

- ❑ is just an idea in my mind...we're learning!

These options are followed by a question:

> *What needs do you think you will have that Marketplace Multipliers can seek to meet?*

With their registration, they are sent a welcome/confirmation letter, and a "Starting a Chapter" guide.

Individual Registration:

Within each chapter, individual MMs will be identified and registered if affiliated with a chapter. We affirm the priority of the Chapter in connecting the MM to their local church and giving them a peer encouragement/accountability/prayer context.

We do not want this to be a movement disconnected from the local church, but also realize for many reasons a MM may not be connected to a local church. This allows for a connection for those who may not be where a local church chapter is available for those whose work, or school (college students, etc.) or other life commitments have taken them away from their church. Therefore, individual "membership" is also available to connect individual MMs for resourcing, connecting, and encouraging.

Lastly, individual membership may prove beneficial for marketplace multipliers who are engaged in their church and seek to live an integrated life, but their church and/or pastor has not fully committed to taking concrete actions to launch a chapter. This membership could further equip the MM to strategically support their pastor, feel supported by other MMs in the meantime, and lead their church's progression to eventually launch a MM chapter in partnership with their pastor.

Benefits of individual membership: In addition to the resources available to all, there will be peer learning connections for MMs. Some of these will be opportunities that apply to every MM member. Others will be specialty gatherings based on their workplace context (their "mountains of influence" – health care, government, retail, athletics, etc.) or their roles (owners, customer service, C-suite, hairdressers, etc.). There may well be members who form virtual chapters, meeting online with a group of peers.

Whether it is an individual registration or a chapter registration, the goal remains the same: Whatever their workplace setting, wherever it is in the world, the MM Movement will focus on integrating faith with work and influencing others to fully follow Christ.

STEP 2 – Create an Invitation List

Think of people who have a desire to live out their faith in the workplace. They may be at various places in their own personal spiritual journey and have different levels of involvement in your church. It may help to bring together a few that you know to brainstorm together for others who might be invited. It may be helpful not only to think of those currently in your church, but people in the community, neighborhood, or workplaces.

Many local church chapters have started with those who indicated interest after a message or series on "faith at work." In some cases, series have been shared with the pastor communicating biblical teaching and MMs also sharing. Responses have been gathered through virtual or printed cards or by having people stand or come forward to be prayed for as marketplace multipliers.

STEP 3 – Pray for those being invited

The first thing to do with your list is to pray over the names, asking God to prompt those who He would desire to be responsive to your invitation. It could be meaningful to turn a Scripture passage into a prayer for the names on your list, such as Hebrews 10:19-25:

Thank You, Lord, for salvation through Jesus Christ and that our Savior prays for us and those we are inviting. May we draw near to God our Father to have our hearts cleansed and our hope fortified. May our MM chapter be a place to consider how we can spur one another on to love and good work in our marketplace settings. May our meetings be a place of encouragement, and where together we experience the empowerment of your Spirit." Amen.

STEP 4 – Partner with others

The primary partnership in a chapter is between a pastor and MM in your local church. This models the complementary roles of lay and clergy, distributes the responsibilities, and supports consistency in the meetings even if a leader needs to be absent.

Some have created a small team to organize and implement the quarterly meetings and to represent various marketplace contexts, voices, and roles.

STEP 5 – Plan your quarterly meetings

Some chapters start with a big event, but most chapters start simply. While most use the Marketplace Multipliers name, you may want to call your group something else. Practical considerations include deciding where to meet. Details might include whether to serve refreshments, make name tags, etc. Consider the best time for the meetings. Seek to schedule at least a couple of meetings in advance so people can block their calendar. Ask everyone about meetings times/days work best.

It also helps to have a plan for what the meeting may include:

- Welcome and opening prayer – shared by the pastor and MM partner.

- Participants sharing about their workplace and their own role in it. In smaller groups, everyone might share. In larger groups choose a few to share at each quarterly meeting. It may include examples of how they are seeking to integrate their faith with their work and be a spiritual influence on others. Usually, it works best to ask people in advance and have them plan to share for 5 minutes or so.

- Presentation from someone in the group or an invited guest on a workplace topic. Some groups utilize video presentations.

- They may be encouraged to read an article or book before the next quarterly chapter meeting.

- In the closing prayer time they might break into smaller groups or pair off, share prayer requests, and pray for each other. Encourage their prayer requests to be specific in how they are seeking to integrate their faith with their work, or for a person they are discipling or influencing. More general prayer requests are fine, but often can be shared in many places. Specific prayer requests related to the marketplace they serve to remind them that the real action is in the workplace.

- Ask them to commit to the next meeting time and invite someone else to come with them.

STEP 6 – Contact your list

The more personal the invitation, the better. It may be a face-to-face invite, a phone call, or personal text or email. Announcements in church or posts on social media may prompt a few to participate, but individualized invites are best. Give each person the specific start and end times, address, and a sense of what the gathering will feel like. Let them know you really would like them to participate and how you already see them as a marketplace influecer and thus a marketplace multiplier.

STEP 7 – Hold your first meeting

Note who attended, what worked well and what can be improved. Don't put pressure on yourself or others to get it perfect the first time. Do your best and then rest in the fact you have taken action. Practice makes perfect. Experience is a great teacher and little adjustments can make a big difference. Feedback from participants could help you understand what they appreciated most and could perhaps be a greater focus in meetings to come.

Start simple and just start. Don't get stuck on the launch being elaborate or perfect. And have your next meeting scheduled.

The meetings are important, but not the

end goal. What makes a person a MM is not that they attend the meeting, but they represent Christ well in the marketplace and as a result there are more followers of Jesus. How they start helps set the trajectory for what they will become.

Pastor Tim Fox led Hydrant Church, a fruitful disciple-making congregation in Goldsboro, North Carolina. He has a special calling to equip smaller churches through his *ReThink Small* equipping and coaching initiative. He has been an early adopter of the MM vision and recognizes its potential for a church of any size. Pastor Tim partnered with Jason Brice, a MM who is an influencer in their church family and the community.

On Labor Day of 2020, Tim launched a two-part series on *work as worship* (glorifying God through Christlike character and excellence in the workplace) and *work as mission* (a context to form relationships that lead to more disciples). He extended the opportunity for congregants to be part of the launch of the Hydrant MM chapter. The third weekend as a culmination of the series they met for the first time.

He texted us a picture of their first gathering of five women and men. Accompanying the picture was this text message, "Our first gathering of multipliers. We shared stories, heard a teaching on your 'why' from Jason, started a shared group chat for connection and support, and prayed together. Each one committed to bring another next time."

Pastor Brian Blum leads Frontline Church, a larger congregation in Grand Rapids, Michigan with multiple campuses in their network. His MM partner is Pat Young, who is respected within the Church but also well networked beyond the Church. Among Pat's connections is a business owner named Tom Darby who for years has been intentional about marketplace ministry and has authored the book *Marketplace*

Missionaries.[9] Pat found the book to be "a great resource for me to get my head wrapped around what God was wanting." So, Pat invited Tom to speak at the launch of their MM chapter. Other chapters have utilized bringing in a guest to provide inspiration and insight to those MMs who may connect with their chapter.

Pastor Irving Figueroa leads the El Taller Church in Guyanbo, a suburb of San Juan, Puerto Rico. El Taller is a multi-economic congregation. Many of the key influencers throughout the island are part of the church. These influencers work in business, government, education, media and more – so they seek to honor Christ in a wide variety of contexts. Well prior to the introduction of their MM chapter, Pastor Irving organized periodic speaker events with a broad outreach to the city. He envisions the MM chapter hosting these outreach opportunities annually or

---

[9] Tom Darby, *Marketplace Missionaries: Where Will Your Coworkers Spend Eternity,* 2020.

semi-annually and in between having more interactive MM chapter meetings.

In summary, while every chapter has its own unique "start story" there are some common elements in the vast majority of these starts. Here is the common thread we are seeing in most chapters:

- There is a recognition of the compelling need to move disciple making beyond the walls of the church and an affirmation of the potential of the marketplace for people to let the light of Christ shine through their everyday lives.

- There is a vision cast by a pastor and/or MM that awakens others to the calling every believer has upon their lives to be good news in the lives of others and to share that good news through opportunities created in the marketplace.

- A partnership develops between a pastor and MM enabling them to collaborate to create a regular opportunities for MMs to spur one another on.

- They register their chapter in order to connect with a broader movement of other MMs, pastors, and churches.

- They start a chapter that reflects the variety
  of marketplace roles in their church and
  community. The chapter is not just for
  men or just for women. It's not only one
  age group. It seeks to include the variety of
  ethnicities represented in the workplaces
  of their community. It includes people of
  various financial means and circumstances.
  It is white collar and blue collar. Beginning
  this way is important because it is difficult
  to start with just one type of MM and then
  seek to diversify later. Some larger chapters
  do develop specialized gatherings or even
  do some breakouts during the quarterly
  meetings of the chapter to connect people
  with similar roles or those in similar
  workplace contexts. But the highest potential
  chapters start as a microcosm of their
  churches and communities.

In the growing MM movement, we're
creating peer learning opportunities on a
continual basis related to identifying and
recruiting leaders for this ministry. We've
created a document "Starting Your Own
Chapter" that is sent to people when a chapter
is registered.

CHAPTER EIGHT

Equipping Marketplace Multipliers

We are thankful for the incredible number of resources available on websites, writings (books, articles, blogs, etc.) and digital resources (videos, online conferences and webinars, etc.) that have helped us create a MM Movement amongst Wesleyans. When it comes to MM resourcing for local church movements/chapters, there are three key concepts that we have identified as a guide to our vision for equipping MMs: connecting, curating and creating.

Connecting

First and foremost, we believe in the power of peer learning. Its potential and impact is often overlooked because of the abundance of more "packaged" resources, but this personal and relational approach to learning is both ancient and relevant today. Additionally, since the calling of a MM is highly relational, it only makes sense for the MM equipping and connecting to be highly relational, too.

The wisdom literature of the Old Testament speaks of its value in Proverbs: "As iron sharpens iron, so one person sharpens another" (27:17) and "Plans fail for lack of counsel, but with many advisors they succeed" (15:22).

The wisdom of Ecclesiastes pronounces "Two are better than one, because they have a good return for this work…" (4:9). That "return" can be measured in productivity and profitability, but also eternal rewards as well. The passage specifically mentions the benefit of recovery from failure (4:10). Failure has a way of deepening our personal faith, and those around us are certainly watching to see how we respond in the face of failure. Connecting with others can be the key to moving failure from being final to being fruitful – a lesson that makes us better.

There is also the "warmth" of relationships mentioned in Ecclesiastes (4:11) that keep us from cold-hearted cynicism that undermines our influence. When we become critical of others and constantly complain about our workplace, people we desire to spiritually influence begin to distance themselves from us. But when we warmly relate to others and are people of "Good News" there can be an attractiveness that ultimately draws people to Christ. The final benefit of peer relationships mentioned in this passage is the protection and even empowerment that comes from working with and learning from others (4:12). To walk with someone who has our back, but also tells us what we need to hear, strengthening us for whatever challenges may come.

Peer learning is essential within local church movements/chapters. This certainly parallels the type of learning that takes place within an Expedition Team.[10] Sometimes it is done by identifying a person within the chapter who gives a presentation about their workplace, their role in it and what they are learning as they seek to integrate their faith and steward their influence. At other times, it is accomplished as people share prayer requests and celebrate ways in which they see God at work in them and through them in their marketplace. Many groups include a time when someone with a particular expertise they've developed or a unique experience they've had that would benefit other MMs. In most local MM chapter meetings, interaction is a priority because of the insight and encouragement it provides to "spur one another on toward love and good deeds" (Hebrews 10:24).

In the broader MM movement, pastors and MMs from various chapters are in virtual learning groups. This is similar to a Caravan,

---

[10] greatestexpedition.com

where five or so Expedition Teams come together for support, cross-learning, coaching, and accountability. These connections facilitate peer learning around different dimensions of building a MM movement/ chapter or being a MM personally.

Earlier this year, a Zoom group convened to share ideas from a variety of churches on starting a MM chapter. About a dozen chapters were represented in calls that we (Ken and Carrie) have hosted. We identified two local church chapters to share their "start stories" (about 7 minutes each). It was followed by *all on the call* allowing chapters to tell their own start stories.

Within the same week another Zoom group convened for peer learning about equipping MMs for integrating their faith and stewarding their influence in the marketplace. The same format was utilized, but the focus of the peer learning experience was unique. Twenty chapters were represented in this call.

This chapter-to-chapter connecting for

learning may sometimes be general. Other times, they may discuss specific items, such as how chapters are using a particular resource. All the connections are designed with the focus of MMs getting beyond the walls of the Church to make disciples in the marketplace.

Curating

This can be defined as "to pull together, sift through, and select for presentation." When it comes to MM resources, the abundance of options can quickly overwhelm those who are seeking the right study guide, book, or video series. We always want to affirm the primacy of Scripture in providing authoritative guidance in integrating our faith with our work and in stewarding our influence in the marketplace in order to make disciples. Biblical principles and stories are an eternally impactful resource as God's living and active Word takes root in our lives.

As a MM movement we are not primarily focused on the creation of resources. We are grateful for the numerous resources available and recommend their use, but regularly remind ourselves that reading books or consuming media is a means to an end. Our primary focus is mobilization for the multiplication of disciples in the marketplace.

As the movement expands, the number of MMs multiply, and chapters grow, we'll learn which widely-available resources people are finding to be especially helpful. Our website identifies some of those resources. This won't replace the need for each chapter to discern the resources that will be most beneficial to them, but as we curate, we seek to focus the search so overload doesn't overwhelm chapter leaders and participants. A list of recommended resources can be found on our MM website.[11]

There are two main resources we feel are foundational to MMs getting started to equip them for integrating their faith in their daily work (Barna's *Christians at Work*)[12] and stewarding their influence (*9 Arts*).[13]

When it comes to *integrating* one's faith with his or her work, we have found Barna's "*Christians at Work*: *Examining the intersection of calling and career*" to be a helpful framework. It addresses the myth of sacred vs. secular jobs, and seeks to answer the question "How do we integrate faith and work?"

Barna's study explores how people experience a sense of purpose through their professional lives, with a close look at the Christians who appear to successfully integrate their faith and their work. It is a research project, providing key findings at a glance for those not prone to dig into the research methodologies. In a spectrum of Faith-Work integration, three vocational personalities are defined among Christian workers:

---

[12] https://www.barna.com/christiansatwork/

[13] https://the9arts.com/

- 34% were "compartmentalizers" (pragmatic employees without strong connections to their faith or work)

- 38% were "onlookers" (passive employees positioned to better connect their faith with their work)

- 28% were "integrators" (enthusiastic employees deeply connected to their faith and their work)." It is helpful for MM to understand these "vocational personalities" when it comes to being a MM.

When it comes to *influencing* others in the marketplace, *The 9 Arts of Spiritual Conversations* website (www.the9arts.com) provides an assessment to identify areas of strength that will help you talk about God with anyone. The 9 Arts of spiritual conversations are identified as noticing, praying, listening, asking questions, loving, welcoming, facilitating, serving together, and sharing. *The 9 Arts Books and Small Group Guides* can be purchased from their website. Their core conviction is that every conversation about God starts with a relational connection, and that *The 9 Arts of Spiritual Conversations*, modeled by Jesus, will help you talk about God with anyone.

Creating

We believe there is great value in *connecting* MMs for peer learning – our mantra is "connect over create." Next, we strive to increase awareness of the variety of marketplace multiplication resources made available through others, and to identify those we believe to be foundational and most helpful – to *curate*. We're appreciative of the opportunity through *The Greatest Expedition* to share this resource created for churches who seek to make disciples through a movement of marketplace multipliers. It was specifically designed for the Expedition Teams and we affirm the value of pastor and lay people journeying together!

We have also created a Marketplace Multipliers book (available in English and Spanish) which is a compilation of stories about

MMs who are seeking to integrate their faith with their work and be a spiritual influence in their marketplace. It contains 17 short stories about a variety of people in a variety of places. It is designed so it can also be shared with others, bookmarking the couple of stories the giver believes will be most relevant to the person receiving the gift.[14]

For inspirational stories of marketplace multipliers, visit anchor.fm/marketplacemultipliers. Periodically, you will hear a story of how a MM is integrating their faith with their everyday work. The inspirational story also features the MMs pastor providing a brief affirmation of that MM in particular and the movement in general. You can see that even in the resources we create we feature a peer learning approach by sharing the stories of MMs, believing they will be a source of inspiration and insight to benefit others. MM movements/chapters affirm the value of peer

---

[14] Marketplace Multipliers: Stories of Faith and Influence in the Marketplace available at wesleyan.org/wph

learning and the sharing of experiences among the participants. So, they utilize more formal equipping resources in a way that informs that peer learning without marginalizing it.

Following are some examples of how different MMs chapters are using resources to equip and encourage their MMs:

Earl McJett is a MM who partners with Pastor Michael Rogalski at LifePoint Church in Waldorf, Maryland is teaching *The 9 Arts of Spiritual Conversations*. Earl works in the U.S. federal government where there are significant regulations and guidelines related to sharing one's faith. But he also wants the Good News to be shared and finds *The 9 Arts* to be a helpful way of appropriately entering relationships in his workplace environment and to develop further interest in spiritual conversations beyond the workplace context. They offer *The 9 Arts* seminar periodically as a complement to their chapter meetings.

Reneé Berg teaches art in public middle school. Outside of school hours she leads

Bible studies for teachers every other week.
One group meets by Zoom. The other group
meets in person. During one meeting, the
group focuses on the study. In the alternate
week each connects with their "buddy for
the study." These 6-part studies are offered
a couple of times a year. She also utilizes
her teaching gift within her local church at
Mitchell Wesleyan Church in Mitchell, South
Dakota in partnership with Discipleship
Pastor Bryan Pohlen. When launching their
MM chapter, they designed a MM orientation
class for teaching and discussing the biblical
foundations and best practices of integrating
faith with work and being a spiritual influence.
This approach fit well with the discipleship
course structure of their local church.

Debbye Turner Bell is a veterinarian.
Soon after being crowned Miss America, she
embarked on a career in communication,
media, and consulting. She is a leader who
has partnered with Lead Pastor Mick Veach at
Kentwood Community Church in Kentwood,

Michigan to design a comprehensive curriculum for Christ-centered leadership. This course is separate complements their MM chapter meetings.

Pastor Wes Coffey leads a church at GracePointe Church in Owosso, Michigan that is a host site for the annual Global Leadership Network conference. They utilize not only the excellent teaching during the annual conference, but its video resources have been helpful in equipping MMs for marketplace effectiveness. The video resources are also very accessible for those who are currently exploring a commitment to Christ as well as those well along in their spiritual journeys.

These are just a few examples of chapters using resources they have either created or selected for equipping MMs. Some are conducted as multi-week classes, others are held periodically. In some cases, they are focused on participants in the MM chapters. In other cases, the resources are offered more widely to the church and the community.

CHAPTER NINE

Marketplace Multipliers and the Congregational Connection

The culture of the congregation is critical to the flourishing of a disciple-making movement beyond the walls of the Church. Research indicates most congregations in North America have plateaued or are declining. As congregations struggle with this reality, a "scarcity" mindset can set in and attention is given almost exclusively to what is needed to survive. The unintended consequence can be an internal focus and the energy of the church is invested in the activities within its walls and the preferences of those who are already committed.

We are often asked if there is a certain size recommendation for a church to have a flourishing Marketplace Multiplier ministry.

It is not the size of the attendance or budget that matters for a church to have a flourishing marketplace multiplication movement. Churches from micro to mega are engaged in disciple-making. It is the size of the church's heart, the willingness to be blessers, to be senders of people beyond its walls so the Gospel spreads, and the resulting transformed lives that really matter. It is a generosity or abundance mindset rather than a scarcity mindset. Ironically, it is when a church blesses that it is blessed. What is invested for the sake of the Kingdom does not diminish its sustainability but builds its Kingdom capacity. These are the attributes of churches having the culture that support and encourage a MM movement.

As a church disciples its congregants, MMs are identified, recruited, equipped, and deployed. The MM continues to live out their discipleship through congregational worship, continued involvement in a discipleship growth group, stewardship, prayer, being in the Word daily, etc. As part of the discipleship journey the MM is on, the MM serves as a disciple by integrating their faith and their work and influencing others in their workplace. The church serves as preparation for MMs, a launch pad for MMs, continuously equipping the MMs, and a source of encouragement and support for MMs. Likewise, the church is experiencing greater Kingdom impact because of the launching of the MM movement. It is a win-win for all!

If in the pastoral or congregational prayer time there is prayer for the spiritual influence of those in their marketplace contexts, it enlarges the church's heart and vision for people in their mission field. If those who give of their time are not only celebrated as volunteers within the church walls, but "missionaries" beyond the church walls, the MMs feel even more connected to their church and committed to its mission. In addition, this may also plant seeds for those who may be considering becoming a MM.

There are many practical ways a congregation can support the ministry of its members beyond the walls of the church. Including the MM movement in prayer times has already been mentioned. Sharing stories or testimonies of what is happening as people live out their faith in the marketplace can be an inspiration to others. An annual "sending" service can highlight the value of the congregation going/sending, as well as gathering.

Congregations where there is a broader value placed upon the "priesthood of all believers" are particularly conducive to the blessing and sending of MMs. Pastor Steve DeNeff partners with Eric Crisp in the MM ministry of their local church. Steve is coauthor with David Drury of the book *SoulShift*[15] which emphasizes the transformative transitions Christians make in their discipleship journeys. One of those shifts is "sheep to shepherd."

As one MM who is general manager of a

---

[15] Steve DeNeff and David Drury, *Soulshift: Measure of the Life Transformed*, Wesleyan Publishing House, 2012.

hotel property said, "I believe I'm a 'pastor' to the 300-plus employees of this hotel. I want them to know they are cared for and that their work is significant, and I want them to know it is not just because I'm a good boss. It's because of the difference Jesus has made in my life."

CHAPTER TEN

Leadership Needed for the Movement

So much depends on leadership. Pastors are the primary blessers and senders in most congregations. But key lay leaders who serve on the local church's governing board and in other ministry areas are essential blessers and senders as well. A church's culture generally reflects its leadership. When that leadership sees the MM initiative as an extension of its disciple-making ministry, it energizes those seeking to integrate their faith and be spiritual influences in their marketplaces.

Beyond the local church, leaders play a significant role regionally and globally. One of the most significant mobilizers in our MM movement is the judicatory leader of the

Great Lakes Region of The Wesleyan Church, Chris Conrad. Chris partners with a close MM friend, Dave Gerry, to visit about ten churches a year to cast the MM vision. Chris has repeatedly stated that he dreams of the day when there are not just two significant weekends (Christmas and Easter) in the life of the local church, but a third weekend, dedicated to the sending of marketplace multipliers. His influence has resulted in many churches having an annual "Sending Sunday" for the commissioning of disciple makers beyond the walls of the Church.

When Chris and Dave share their MM vision with a local church, those present are sure to hear their sense of urgency and commitment to the Great Commission, along with sharing about how the marketplace has been significant as a context for the sharing of the Gospel.

Chris affirms how Dave's influence in Madison, Wisconsin has made a city-wide difference in churches, businesses and community organizations. Dave has a particular gift for intercession, and always gives an opportunity for people to be prayed over as ministers in their marketplaces. This has been transformational for many, as they come to recognize their workplace ministry as their calling.

Global leadership has been significant. Marketplace Multipliers launched as a global movement. Early in its development, two MMs presented the vision by webinar to a variety of leaders across the Asia-Pacific region. Leaders in North America partnered with leaders throughout Iberoamerica in order to spread the MM disciple-making vision to Spanish-speakers around the world. It has been exciting to see MM movement grow across the globe.

Contextualization is a key value in all expressions of the Church. A judicatory leader can be a great help as churches do this important contextualization. A local MM movement/chapter must determine what fits its church in order to make disciples in its community. A regional judicatory recognizes and customizes the MM vision presentation to the unique cultural aspects of its geographical area. Globally, Spanish-speakers met multiple times to contextualize the MM strategy for Latin culture. This went beyond simply translating MM materials into Spanish, but realizing what needed to be emphasized and affirmed in the pastor/lay relationship, in the church/marketplace contexts for disciple-making, and in other dimensions of the MM convening and sending.

The complexity of contextualization in the Asia-Pacific region became immediately apparent. Many countries have largely day-labor economies, such as Bangladesh and India. Others have complex economic systems such as Singapore, China, Australia, and New Zealand. The shape of the economy in a country impacts the shape of the MM disciple-making in that country.

As General Superintendent of the North American General Conference of The

Wesleyan Church, I (Wayne) have a platform to cast the MM vision. Our denomination places high value on both laity and clergy, which provides a supportive context for a significant investment in connecting with judicatory leaders and influential local churches to fan the flames of the MM movement.

Conclusion

I (Carrie) continue to humbly pray for
God's holy presence and intercession in our
local churches, communities, and world.
Following a global pandemic, there is no
better time than the present to instill hope
and spread love everywhere, including the
workplace. There is no better time to dig deep
into our hearts, souls, and minds to exude
Holy Spirit-filled compassion and empathy to
all we encounter within and outside the walls
of the church.

We need to wholeheartedly reflect on
how we are best using our gifts of time and
talent to optimize our influence, integrating
our faith and making disciples, whether at
home or in our work environment. We must

be encouraged and empowered to urgently deploy and boldly act in highly intentional ways that unleash God's kingdom and awaken all Christians to serve as a multiplier of Christ in their vocation. I can imagine a world where we all know Jesus, we all know our purpose to serve Him and we all know how to turn that purpose into action.

I (Wayne) am so incredibly grateful for the opportunity to support and encourage the MMs who are leading this movement and to celebrate the pastors who are blessing and sending those MMs. In an intriguing way, having a part in awakening MMs for their calling in the marketplace renews my appreciation for my own calling.

Years ago, while serving as a local church pastor, I was challenged with this statement – "most pastors want more *from* people in the marketplace than they want *for* people in the marketplace." This layperson observed that it felt like many pastors view business as a regrettably necessary "secular" activity, allowing people to make money to support the "spiritual" ministry of the church. When I got over my initial defensiveness, I was convicted by that thought and motivated to want more *for* people in the marketplace.

Generosity in giving is something I want for all of us. As Jesus put it, "Where your treasure is, there your heart will be also" (Matthew 6:21).

"You cannot serve both God and money" (Matthew 6:24). Our stewardship of money is not ultimately a financial matter, but is of spiritual and eternal significance. It is as essential to being a disciple as reading the Bible, praying and other activities that develop spiritual maturity. But I also want everyone to experience the joy of making disciples, of finding significance in the opportunities of their marketplace context, and the incredible blessing of living called and sent every day.

The MM movement is still a mustard seed (Matthew 13:31-32; 17:20-21). By faith we see it being transformative in every person, church and community around the world. We believe it is an answer to the prayer, "Your kingdom come, Your will be done, on earth as it is in heaven" (Matthew 6:10). We find it to be part of *The Greatest Expedition*!

A final thought from Kay Kotan

I continue to be amazed by the faithful methods disciples continue to seek to connect with those who are far from Christ. So much of the effective ministry of reaching people in this post-modern world is a return to the simpler and more relational methods that Jesus taught us during His time on earth. Just like the movement of missional communities, the marketplace multipliers movement is a connection to a more organic and relationally-centered way of connecting new people to Christ.

In a time when the church as a whole is having trouble finding traction, it is the individual disciples who are doing life out and about in the world that will reach people. Being raw, real, and vulnerable as we walk alongside others who are searching for purpose and meaning in their lives. Meeting people where they are. I find great hope and possibility for these movements. I pray God will move mountains so these movements can gain traction, making the Good News the most popular news every day.

What is *The Greatest Expedition*?

The Greatest Expedition is a congregational journey for churches, charges, or cooperative parishes led by a church Expedition Team of 8-12 brave pioneering leaders. The purpose of *The Greatest Expedition* is to provide an experience for Expedition Teams to explore their local context in new ways to develop new MAPS (ministry action plans) so you are more relevant and contextual to reach new people in your community. Updated tools and guides are provided for the church's Expedition Team. Yet, it is a "choose your own adventure" type of journey.

The tools and guides will be provided, but it is up to the church's Expedition Team to decide which tools are needed, which tools just need sharpening, which tools can stay in their backpack to use at a later time, what pathways to explore, and what pathways to pass.

the greatest
EXPEDITION

The Greatest Expedition provides a new lens and updated tools to help your Expedition Team explore and think about being the church in different ways. Will your Expedition Team need to clear the overgrown brush from a once known trail, but not recently traveled? Or will the Expedition Team need to cut a brand new trail with their new tools? Or perhaps, will the Team decide they need to move to a completely fresh terrain and begin breaking ground for something brand new in a foreign climate?

Registration is open and Expedition Teams are launching!

greatestexpedition.com

the greatest
EXPEDITION

These Books Now Available
as resources of
The Greatest Expedition

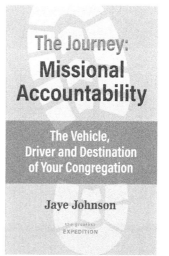

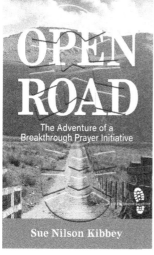

These Books Now Available
as resources of
The Greatest Expedition

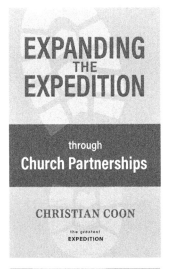

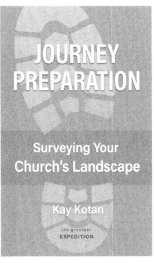

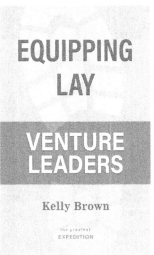

marketsquarebooks.com

Made in the USA
Columbia, SC
01 August 2021